How to Answer
65 of the Toughest Interview
Questions in any Job Industry

By: Kendall Cook

How to Answer 65 of the Toughest Interview Questions in any Job Industry

ISBN-13 978-1-933804-84-2

Printed in the United States of America

Please visit our website at www.itcookbook.com

This book is dedicated to those who need a pep talk
before heading into a job interview

Table of Contents

An Introduction - General Guidelines in Answering Interview Questions

Everyone is nervous on interviews. If you simply allow yourself to feel nervous, you'll do much better. Remember also that it's difficult for the interviewer as well.

In general, be upbeat and positive. Never be negative.

Rehearse your answers and time them. Never talk for more than 2 minutes straight.

Don't try to memorize answers word for word. Use the answers shown here as a guide only, and don't be afraid to include your own thoughts and words. To help you remember key concepts, jot down and review a few key words for each answer. Rehearse your answers frequently, and they will come to you naturally in interviews.

As you will read in the following pages, the single most important strategy in interviewing, as in all phases of your job search, is what we call: "The Greatest Executive Job Finding Secret." And that is...

Find out what people want, than show them how you can help them get it.

Find out what an employer wants most in his or her ideal candidate, then show how you meet those qualifications.

In other words, you must match your abilities, with the needs of the employer. You must sell what the buyer is buying. To do that, before you know what to emphasize in your answers, you must find out what the buyer is buying... what he is looking for. And the best way to do that is to ask a few questions yourself.

You will see how to bring this off skillfully as you read the first two questions of this report. But regardless of how you accomplish it, you must remember this strategy above all: before blurting out your qualifications, you must get some idea of what the employer wants most. Once you know what he wants, you can then present your qualifications as the perfect "key" that fits the "lock" of that position.

Other important interview strategies:

Turn weaknesses into strengths (You'll see how to do this in a few moments.)

Think before you answer. A pause to collect your thoughts is a hallmark of a thoughtful person.

As a daily exercise, practice being more optimistic. For example, try putting a positive spin on events and situations you would normally regard as negative. This is not meant to turn you into a Pollyanna, but to sharpen your selling skills. The best salespeople, as well as the best liked interview candidates, come off as being naturally optimistic, "can do" people. You will dramatically raise your level of attractiveness by daily practicing to be more optimistic.

Be honest...never lie.

Keep an interview diary. Right after each interview note what you did right, what could have gone a little better, and what steps you should take next with this contact. Then take those steps.

About the 65 questions...

You might feel that the answers to the following questions are "canned", and that they will seldom match up with the exact way you are asked the questions in actual interviews. The questions and answers are designed to be as specific and realistic as possible. But no preparation can anticipate thousands of possible variations on these questions. What's important is that you thoroughly familiarize yourself with the main strategies behind each answer. And it will be invaluable to you if you commit to memory a few key words that let you instantly call to mind your best answer to the various questions. If you do this, and follow the principles of successful interviewing presented here, you're going to do very well.

Good luck...and happy job-hunting!

Question 1   Tell me about yourself

TRAPS: Beware; about 80% of all interviews begin with this "innocent" question. Many candidates, unprepared for the question, skewer themselves by rambling, recapping their life story, delving into ancient work history or personal matters.

BEST ANSWER: Start with the present and tell why you are well qualified for the position. Remember that the key to all successful interviewing is to match your qualifications to what the interviewer is looking for. In other words *you must sell what the buyer is buying. This is the single most important strategy in job hunting.*

So, before you answer this or *any* question it's imperative that you try to uncover your interviewer's greatest need, want, problem or goal.

To do so, make you take these two steps:

Do all the homework you can before the interview to uncover *this person's* wants and needs (not the generalized needs of the industry or company)

As early as you can in the interview, ask for a more complete description of what the position entails. You might say: "I have a number of accomplishments I'd like to tell you about, but I want to make the best use of our time together and talk directly to your needs. To help me do, that, could you tell me more about the most important priorities of this position? All I know is what I (heard from the recruiter, read in the classified ad, etc.)"

Then, **ALWAYS** *follow-up with a second and possibly, third question,* to draw out his needs even more. Surprisingly, it's usually this *second* or *third* question that unearths what the interviewer is *most* looking for.

You might ask simply, "And in addition to that?..." or, "Is there anything else you see as essential to success in this position?:

This process will not feel easy or natural at first, because it is easier simply to answer questions, but only if you uncover the employer's wants and needs will your answers make the most sense. Practice asking these key questions before giving your answers, the process will feel more natural *and you will be light years ahead of the other job candidates you're competing with.*

After uncovering what the employer is looking for, describe why the needs of this job bear striking parallels to tasks you've succeeded at before. Be sure to illustrate with specific examples of your responsibilities and especially your achievements, all of which are geared to present yourself as a perfect match for the needs he has just described.

Question 2   What are your greatest strengths?

TRAPS: This question seems like a softball lob, but be prepared. You don't want to come across as egotistical or arrogant. Neither is this a time to be humble.

BEST ANSWER: You know that your key strategy is to first uncover your interviewer's greatest wants and needs before you answer questions. And from Question 1, you know how to do this.

Prior to any interview, you should have a list mentally prepared of your greatest strengths. You should also have, a specific example or two, which illustrates each strength, an example chosen from your most recent and most impressive achievements.

You should, have this list of your greatest strengths and corresponding examples from your achievements so well committed to memory that you can recite them cold after being shaken awake at 2:30AM.

Then, once you uncover your interviewer's greatest wants and needs, you can choose those achievements from your list that best match up.

As a general guideline, the 10 most desirable traits that all employers love to see in their employees are:

A proven track record as an achiever...especially if your achievements match up with the employer's greatest wants and needs.

Intelligence...management "savvy".

Honesty...integrity...a decent human being.

Good fit with corporate culture...someone to feel comfortable with...a team player who meshes well with interviewer's team.

Likeability...positive attitude...sense of humor.

Good communication skills.

Dedication...willingness to walk the extra mile to achieve excellence.

Definiteness of purpose...clear goals.

Enthusiasm...high level of motivation.

Confident...healthy...a leader.

Question 3   What are your greatest weaknesses?

TRAPS: Beware - this is an eliminator question, designed to shorten the candidate list. Any admission of a weakness or fault will earn you an "A" for honesty, but an "F" for the interview.

PASSABLE ANSWER: Disguise strengths as weaknesses.

Example: "I sometimes push my people too hard. I like to work with a sense of urgency and everyone is not always on the same wavelength."

Drawback: This strategy is better than admitting a flaw, but it's so widely used, it is transparent to any experienced interviewer.

BEST ANSWER: (and another reason it's so important to get a thorough description of your interviewer's needs before you answer questions): Assure the interviewer that you can think of nothing that would stand in the way of your performing in this position with excellence. Then, quickly review you strongest qualifications.

Example: "Nobody's perfect, but based on what you've told me about this position, I believe I' d make an outstanding match. I know that when I hire people, I look for two things most of all. Do they have the qualifications to do the job well, and the motivation to do it well? Everything in my background shows I have both the qualifications and a strong desire to achieve excellence in whatever I take on. So I can say in all honesty that I see nothing that would cause you even a small concern about my ability or my strong desire to perform this job with excellence."

Alternate strategy (if you don't yet know enough about the position to talk about such a perfect fit):
Instead of confessing a weakness, describe what you like most and like least, making sure that what you like most matches up with the most important qualification for success in the position, and what you like least is not essential.

Example: Let's say you're applying for a teaching position. "If given a choice, I like to spend as much time as possible in front of my prospects selling, as opposed to shuffling paperwork back at the office. Of course, I long ago learned the importance of filing paperwork properly, and I do it conscientiously. But what I really love to do is sell (if your interviewer were a sales manager, this should be music to his ears.)

Question 4   Tell me about something you did – or failed to do – that you now feel a little ashamed of.

TRAPS: There are some questions your interviewer has no business asking, and this is one. But while you may feel like answering, "none of your business," naturally you can't. Some interviewers ask this question on the chance you admit to something, but if not, at least they'll see how you think on your feet.

Some unprepared candidates, flustered by this question, unburden themselves of guilt from their personal life or career, perhaps expressing regrets regarding a parent, spouse, child, etc. All such answers can be disastrous.

BEST ANSWER: As with faults and weaknesses, never confess a regret. But don't seem as if you're stonewalling either.

Best strategy: Say you harbor no regrets, then add a principle or habit you practice regularly for healthy human relations.

Example: Pause for reflection, as if the question never occurred to you. Then say, "You know, I really can't think of anything." (Pause again, then add): "I would add that as a general management principle, I've found that the best way to avoid regrets is to avoid causing them in the first place. I practice one habit that helps me a great deal in this regard. At the end of each day, I mentally review the day's events and conversations to take a second look at the people and developments I'm involved with and do a doublecheck of what they're likely to be feeling. Sometimes I'll see things that do need more follow-up, whether a pat on the back, or maybe a five minute chat in someone's office to make sure we're clear on things...whatever."

"I also like to make each person feel like a member of an elite team, like the Boston Celtics or LA Lakers in their prime. I've found that if you let each team member know you expect excellence in their performance...if you work hard to set an example yourself...and if you let people know you appreciate and respect their feelings, you wind up with a highly motivated group, a team that's having fun at work because they're striving for excellence rather than brooding over slights or regrets."

Question 5   Why are you leaving (or did you leave) this position?

TRAPS: Never badmouth your previous industry, company, board, boss, staff, employees or customers. This rule is inviolable: never be negative. Any mud you hurl will only soil your suit.

Especially avoid words like "personality clash", "didn't get along", or others which cast a shadow on your competence, integrity, or temperament.

BEST ANSWER:

(If you have a job presently)
If you're not yet 100% committed to leaving your present post, don't be afraid to say so. Since you have a job, you are in a stronger position than someone who does not. But don't be coy either. State honestly what you'd be hoping to find in a new spot. Of course, as stated often before, you answer will all the stronger if you have already uncovered what this position is all about and you match your desires to it.

(If you do not presently have a job.)
Never lie about having been fired. It's unethical – and too easily checked. But do try to deflect the reason from you personally. If your firing was the result of a takeover, merger, division wide layoff, etc., so much the better.

But you should also do something totally unnatural that will demonstrate consummate professionalism. Even if it hurts , describe your own firing – candidly, succinctly and without a trace of bitterness – from the company's point-of-view, indicating that you could understand why it happened and you might have made the same decision yourself.

Your stature will rise immensely and, most important of all, you will show you are healed from the wounds inflicted by the firing.

You will enhance your image as first-class management material and stand head and shoulders above the legions of firing victims who, at the slightest provocation, zip open their shirts to expose their battle scars and decry the unfairness of it all.

For all prior positions:
Make sure you've prepared a brief reason for leaving. Best reasons: more money, opportunity, responsibility or growth.

Question 6   The "Silent Treatment"

TRAPS: Beware – if you are unprepared for this question, you will probably not handle it right and possibly blow the interview. Thank goodness most interviewers don't employ it. It's normally used by those determined to see how you respond under stress. Here's how it works:

You answer an interviewer's question and then, instead of asking another, he just stares at you in a deafening silence.

You wait, growing a bit uneasy, and there he sits, silent as Mt. Rushmore, as if he doesn't believe what you've just said, or perhaps making you feel that you've unwittingly violated some cardinal rule of interview etiquette.

When you get this silent treatment after answering a particularly difficult question , such as "tell me about your weaknesses", its intimidating effect can be most disquieting, even to polished job hunters.

Most unprepared candidates rush in to fill the void of silence, viewing prolonged, uncomfortable silences as an invitation to clear up the previous answer which has obviously caused some problem. And that's what they do – ramble on, sputtering more and more information, sometimes irrelevant and often damaging, because they are suddenly playing the role of someone who's goofed and is now trying to recoup. But since the candidate doesn't know where or how he goofed, he just keeps talking, showing how flustered and confused he is by the interviewer's unmovable silence.

BEST ANSWER: Like a primitive tribal mask, the Silent Treatment loses all it power to frighten you once you refuse to be intimidated. If your interviewer pulls it, keep quiet yourself for a while and then ask, with sincere politeness and not a trace of sarcasm, "Is there anything else I can fill in on that point?" That's all there is to it.

Whatever you do, don't let the Silent Treatment intimidate you into talking a blue streak, because you could easily talk yourself out of the position.

Question 7 Why should I hire you?

TRAPS: Believe it or not, this is a killer question because so many candidates are unprepared for it. If you stammer or adlib you've blown it.

BEST ANSWER: By now you can see how critical it is to apply the overall strategy of uncovering the employer's needs before you answer questions. If you know the employer's greatest needs and desires, this question will give you a big leg up over other candidates because you will give him better reasons for hiring you than anyone else is likely to...reasons tied directly to his needs.

Whether your interviewer asks you this question explicitly or not, this is the most important question of your interview because he must answer this question favorably in is own mind before you will be hired. So help him out! Walk through each of the position's requirements as you understand them, and follow each with a reason why you meet that requirement so well.

Example: "As I understand your needs, you are first and foremost looking for someone who can manage the sales and marketing of your book publishing division. As you've said you need someone with a strong background in trade book sales.

This is where I've spent almost all of my career, so I've chalked up 18 years of experience exactly in this area. I believe that I know the right contacts, methods, principles, and successful management techniques as well as any person can in our industry."

"You also need someone who can expand your book distribution channels. In my prior post, my innovative promotional ideas doubled, then tripled, the number of outlets selling our books. I'm confident I can do the same for you."

"You need someone to give a new shot in the arm to your mail order sales, someone who knows how to sell in space and direct mail media. Here, too, I believe I have exactly the experience you need. In the last five years, I've increased our mail order book sales from $600,000 to $2,800,000, and now we're the country's second leading marketer of scientific and medical books by mail." Etc., etc., etc.,

Every one of these selling "couplets" (his need matched by your qualifications) is a touchdown that runs up your score. IT is your best opportunity to outsell your competition.

Question 8   Aren't you overqualified for this position?

TRAPS: The employer may be concerned that you'll grow dissatisfied and leave.

BEST ANSWER: As with any objection, don't view this as a sign of imminent defeat. It's an invitation to teach the interviewer a new way to think about this situation, seeing advantages instead of drawbacks.

Example: "I recognize the job market for what it is – a marketplace. Like any marketplace, it's subject to the laws of supply and demand. So 'overqualified' can be a relative term, depending on how tight the job market is. And right now, it's very tight. I understand and accept that."

"I also believe that there could be very positive benefits for both of us in this match."

"Because of my unusually strong experience in _____ , I could start to contribute right away, perhaps much faster than someone who'd have to be brought along more slowly."

"There's also the value of all the training and years of experience that other companies have invested tens of thousands of dollars to give me. You'd be getting all the value of that without having to pay an extra dime for it. With someone who has yet to acquire that experience, he'd have to gain it on your nickel."

"I could also help you in many things they don't teach at the Harvard Business School. For example...(how to hire, train, motivate, etc.) When it comes to knowing how to work well with people and getting the most out of them, there's just no substitute for what you learn over many years of front-line experience. You company would gain all this, too."

"From my side, there are strong benefits, as well. Right now, I am unemployed. I want to work, very much, and the position you have here is exactly what I love to do and am best at. I'll be happy doing this work and that's what matters most to me, a lot more that money or title."

"Most important, I'm looking to make a long term commitment in my career now. I've had enough of job-hunting and want a permanent spot at this point in my career. I also know that if I perform this job with excellence, other opportunities cannot help but open up for me right here. In time, I'll find many other ways to help this company and in so doing, help myself. I really am looking to make a long-term commitment."

NOTE: The main concern behind the "overqualified" question is that you will leave your new employer as soon as something better comes your way. Anything you can say to demonstrate the sincerity of your commitment to the employer and reassure him that you're looking to stay for the long-term will help you overcome this objection.

Question 9 Where do you see yourself five years from now?

TRAPS: One reason interviewers ask this question is to see if you're settling for this position, using it merely as a stopover until something better comes along. Or they could be trying to gauge your level of ambition.

If you're too specific, i.e., naming the promotions you someday hope to win, you'll sound presumptuous. If you're too vague, you'll seem rudderless.

BEST ANSWER: Reassure your interviewer that you're looking to make a long-term commitment...that this position entails exactly what you're looking to do and what you do extremely well. As for your future, you believe that if you perform each job at hand with excellence, future opportunities will take care of themselves.

Example: "I am definitely interested in making a long-term commitment to my next position. Judging by what you've told me about this position, it's exactly what I'm looking for and what I am very well qualified to do. In terms of my future career path, I'm confident that if I do my work with excellence, opportunities will inevitable open up for me. It's always been that way in my career, and I'm confident I'll have similar opportunities here."

Question 10 Describe your ideal company, location and job.

TRAPS: This is often asked by an experienced interviewer who thinks you may be overqualified, but knows better than to show his hand by posing his objection directly. So he'll use this question instead, which often gets a candidate to reveal that, indeed, he or she is looking for something other than the position at hand.

BEST ANSWER: The only right answer is to describe what this company is offering, being sure to make your answer believable with specific reasons, stated with sincerity, why each quality represented by this opportunity is attractive to you.

Remember that if you're coming from a company that's the leader in its field or from a glamorous or much admired company, industry, city or position, your interviewer and his company may well have an "Avis" complex. That is, they may feel a bit defensive about being "second best" to the place you're coming from, worried that you may consider them bush league.

This anxiety could well be there even though you've done nothing to inspire it. You must go out of your way to assuage such anxiety, even if it's not expressed, by putting their virtues high on the list of exactly what you're looking for, providing credible reason for wanting these qualities.

If you do not express genuine enthusiasm for the firm, its culture, location, industry, etc., you may fail to answer this "Avis" complex objection and, as a result, leave the interviewer suspecting that a hot shot like you, coming from a Fortune 500 company in New York, just wouldn't be happy at an unknown manufacturer based in Topeka, Kansas.

Question 11 *Why do you want to work at our company?*

TRAPS: This question tests whether you've done any homework about the firm. If you haven't, you lose. If you have, you win big.

BEST ANSWER: This question is your opportunity to hit the ball out of the park, thanks to the in-depth research you should do before any interview.

Best sources for researching your target company: annual reports, the corporate newsletter, contacts you know at the company or its suppliers, advertisements, articles about the company in the trade press.

Question 12 *What are your career options right now?*

TRAPS: The interviewer is trying to find out, "How desperate are you?"

BEST ANSWER: Prepare for this question by thinking of how you can position yourself as a desired commodity. If you are still working, describe the possibilities at your present firm and why, though you're greatly appreciated there, you're looking for something more (challenge, money, responsibility, etc.). Also mention that you're seriously exploring opportunities with one or two other firms.

If you're not working, you can talk about other employment possibilities you're actually exploring. But do this with a light touch, speaking only in general terms. You don't want to seem manipulative or coy.

Question 13 Why have you been out of work so long?

TRAPS: A tough question if you've been on the beach a long time. You don't want to seem like damaged goods.

BEST ANSWER: You want to emphasize factors which have prolonged your job search by your own choice.

Example: "After my job was terminated, I made a conscious decision not to jump on the first opportunities to come along. In my life, I've found out that you can always turn a negative into a positive IF you try hard enough. This is what I determined to do. I decided to take whatever time I needed to think through what I do best, what I most want to do, where I'd like to do it...and then identify those companies that could offer such an opportunity."

"Also, in all honesty, you have to factor in the recession (consolidation, stabilization, etc.) in the (banking, financial services, manufacturing, advertising, etc.) industry."

"So between my being selective and the companies in our industry downsizing, the process has taken time. But in the end, I'm convinced that when I do find the right match, all that careful evaluation from both sides of the desk will have been well worthwhile for both the company that hires me and myself.

Question 14 Tell me honestly about the strong points and weak points of your boss (company, management team, etc.)...

TRAPS: Skillfull interviewers sometimes make it almost irresistible to open up and air a little dirty laundry from your previous position. DON'T

BEST ANSWER: Remember the rule: Never be negative. Stress only the good points, no matter how charmingly you're invited to be critical.

Your interviewer doesn't care a whit about your previous boss. He wants to find out how loyal and positive you are, and whether you'll criticize him behind his back if pressed to do so by someone in this own company. This question is your opportunity to demonstrate your loyalty to those you work with.

Question 15 What good books have you read lately?

TRAPS: As in all matters of your interview, never fake familiarity you don't have. Yet you don't want to seem like a dullard who hasn't read a book since Tom Sawyer.

BEST ANSWER: Unless you're up for a position in academia or as book critic for The New York Times, you're not expected to be a literary lion. But it wouldn't hurt to have read a handful of the most recent and influential books in your profession and on management.

Consider it part of the work of your job search to read up on a few of these leading books. But make sure they are quality books that reflect favorably upon you, nothing that could even remotely be considered superficial. Finally, add a recently published bestselling work of fiction by a world-class author and you'll pass this question with flying colors.

Question 16 *Tell me about a situation when your work was criticized.*

TRAPS: This is a tough question because it's a more clever and subtle way to get you to admit to a weakness. You can't dodge it by pretending you've never been criticized. Everybody has been. Yet it can be quite damaging to start admitting potential faults and failures that you'd just as soon leave buried.

This question is also intended to probe how well you accept criticism and direction.

BEST ANSWERS: Begin by emphasizing the extremely positive feedback you've gotten throughout your career and (if it's true) that your performance reviews have been uniformly excellent.

Of course, no one is perfect and you always welcome suggestions on how to improve your performance. Then, give an example of a not-too-damaging learning experience from early in your career and relate the ways this lesson has since helped you. This demonstrates that you learned from the experience and the lesson is now one of the strongest breastplates in your suit of armor.

If you are pressed for a criticism from a recent position, choose something fairly trivial that in no way is essential to your successful performance. Add that you've learned from this, too, and over the past several years/months, it's no longer an area of concern because you now make it a regular practice to...etc.

Another way to answer this question would be to describe your intention to broaden your master of an area of growing importance in your field. For example, this might be a computer program you've been meaning to sit down and learn... a new management technique you've read about...or perhaps attending a seminar on some cutting-edge branch of your profession.

Again, the key is to focus on something not essential to your brilliant performance but which adds yet another dimension to your already impressive knowledge base.

Question 17 *What are your outside interests/hobbies?*

TRAPS: You want to be a well-rounded, not a drone. But your potential employer would be even more turned off if he suspects that your heavy extracurricular load will interfere with your commitment to your work duties.

BEST ANSWERS: Try to gauge how this company's culture would look upon your favorite outside activities and be guided accordingly.

You can also use this question to shatter any stereotypes that could limit your chances. If you're over 50, for example, describe your activities that demonstrate physical stamina. If you're young, mention an activity that connotes wisdom and institutional trust, such as serving on the board of a popular charity.

But above all, remember that your employer is hiring your for what you can do for him, not your family, yourself or outside organizations, no matter how admirable those activities may be.

Question 18 The "Fatal Flaw" question

TRAPS: If an interviewer has read your resume carefully, he may try to zero in on a "fatal flaw" of your candidacy, perhaps that you don't have a college degree...you've been out of the job market for some time...you never earned your CPA, etc.

A fatal flaw question can be deadly, but usually only if you respond by being overly defensive.

BEST ANSWERS: As every master salesperson knows, you will encounter objections (whether stated or merely thought) in every sale. They're part and parcel of the buyer's anxiety. The key is not to exacerbate the buyer's anxiety but diminish it. Here's how...

Whenever you come up against a fatal flaw question:

Be completely honest, open and straightforward about admitting the shortcoming. (Showing you have nothing to hide diminishes the buyer's anxiety.)

Do not apologize or try to explain it away. You know that this supposed flaw is nothing to be concerned about, and this is the attitude you want your interviewer to adopt as well.

Add that as desirable as such a qualification might be, its lack has made you work all the harder throughout your career and has not prevented you from compiling an outstanding tack record of achievements. You might even give examples of how, through a relentless commitment to excellence, you have consistently outperformed those who do have this qualification.

Of course, the ultimate way to handle "fatal flaw" questions is to prevent them from arising in the first place. You will do that by following the master strategy described in Question 1, i.e., uncovering the employers needs and them matching your qualifications to those needs.

Once you've gotten the employer to start talking about his most urgently-felt wants and goals for the position, and then help him see in step-by-step fashion how perfectly your background and achievements match up with those needs, you're going to have one very enthusiastic interviewer on your hands, one who is no longer looking for "fatal flaws".

Question 19 How do you feel about reporting to a younger person (minority, woman, etc)?

TRAPS: It's a shame that some interviewers feel the need to ask this question, but many understand the reality that prejudices still exist among some job candidates, and it's better to try to flush them out beforehand.

The trap here is that in today's politically sensitized environment, even a well-intentioned answer can result in planting your foot neatly in your mouth. Avoid anything which smacks of a patronizing or an insensitive attitude, such as "I think they make terrific bosses" or "Hey, some of my best friends are..."

Of course, since almost anyone with an IQ above room temperature will at least try to steadfastly affirm the right answer here, your interviewer will be judging your sincerity most of all. "Do you really feel that way?" is what he or she will be wondering.

So you must make your answer believable and not just automatic. If the firm is wise enough to have promoted peopled on the basis of ability alone, they're likely quite proud of it, and prefer to hire others who will wholeheartedly share their strong sense of fair play.

BEST ANSWER: You greatly admire a company that hires and promotes on merit alone and you couldn't agree more with that philosophy. The age (gender, race, etc.) of the person you report to would certainly make no difference to you.

Whoever has that position has obviously earned it and knows their job well. Both the person and the position are fully deserving of respect. You believe that all people in a company, from the receptionist to the Chairman, work best when their abilities, efforts and feelings are respected and rewarded fairly, and that includes you. That's the best type of work environment you can hope to find.

Question 20   On confidential matters...

TRAPS: When an interviewer presses you to reveal confidential information about a present or former employer, you may feel it's a no-win situation. If you cooperate, you could be judged untrustworthy. If you don't, you may irritate the interviewer and seem obstinate, uncooperative or overly suspicious.

BEST ANSWER: Your interviewer may press you for this information for two reasons.

First, many companies use interviews to research the competition. It's a perfect set-up. Here in their own lair, is an insider from the enemy camp who can reveal prized information on the competition's plans, research, financial condition, etc.

Second, the company may be testing your integrity to see if you can be cajoled or bullied into revealing confidential data.

What to do? The answer here is easy. Never reveal anything truly confidential about a present or former employer. By all means, explain your reticence diplomatically. For example, "I certainly want to be as open as I can about that. But I also wish to respect the rights of those who have trusted me with their most sensitive information, just as you would hope to be able to trust any of your key people when talking with a competitor..."

And certainly you can allude to your finest achievements in specific ways that don't reveal the combination to the company safe.

But be guided by the golden rule. If you were the owner of your present company, would you feel it ethically wrong for the information to be given to your competitors? If so, steadfastly refuse to reveal it.

Remember that this question pits your desire to be cooperative against your integrity. Faced with any such choice, always choose integrity. It is a far more valuable commodity than whatever information the company may pry from you. Moreover, once you surrender the information, your stock goes down. They will surely lose respect for you.

One President we know always presses candidates unmercifully for confidential information. If he doesn't get it, he grows visibly annoyed, relentlessly inquisitive, It's all an act. He couldn't care less about the information. This is his way of testing the candidate's moral fiber. Only those who hold fast are hired.

Question 21 Would you lie for the company?

TRAPS: This another question that pits two values against one another, in this case loyalty against integrity.

BEST ANSWER: Try to avoid choosing between two values, giving a positive statement which covers all bases instead.

Example: "I would never do anything to hurt the company.."

If aggressively pressed to choose between two competing values, always choose personal integrity. It is the most prized of all values.

Question 22 Looking back, what would you do differently in your life?

TRAPS: This question is usually asked to uncover any life-influencing mistakes, regrets, disappointments or problems that may continue to affect your personality and performance.

You do not want to give the interviewer anything negative to remember you by, such as some great personal or career disappointment, even long ago, that you wish could have been avoided.

Nor do you wish to give any answer which may hint that your whole heart and soul will not be in your work.

BEST ANSWER: Indicate that you are a happy, fulfilled, optimistic person and that, in general, you wouldn't change a thing.

Example: "It's been a good life, rich in learning and experience, and the best it yet to come. Every experience in life is a lesson it its own way. I wouldn't change a thing."

Question 23 Could you have done better in your last job?

TRAPS: This is no time for true confessions of major or even minor problems.

BEST ANSWER: Again never be negative.

Example: "I suppose with the benefit of hindsight you can always find things to do better, of course, but off the top of my head, I can't think of anything of major consequence."

(If more explanation seems necessary)
Describer a situation that didn't suffer because of you but from external conditions beyond your control.

For example, describe the disappointment you felt with a test campaign, new product launch, merger, etc., which looked promising at first, but led to underwhelming results. "I wish we could have known at the start what we later found out (about the economy turning, the marketplace changing, etc.), but since we couldn't, we just had to go for it. And we did learn from it..."

Question 24 Can you work under pressure?

TRAPS: An easy question, but you want to make your answer believable.

BEST ANSWER: Absolutely...(then prove it with a vivid example or two of a goal or project accomplished under severe pressure.)

Question 25 What makes you angry?

TRAPS: You don't want to come across either as a hothead or a wimp.

BEST ANSWER: Give an answer that's suited to both your personality and the management style of the firm. Here, the homework you've done about the company and its style can help in your choice of words.

Examples: *If you are a reserved person and/or the corporate culture is coolly professional:*

"I'm an even-tempered and positive person by nature, and I believe this helps me a great deal in keeping my department running smoothly, harmoniously and with a genuine esprit de corps. I believe in communicating clearly what's expected, getting people's commitment to those goals, and then following up continuously to check progress."

"If anyone or anything is going off track, I want to know about it early. If, after that kind of open communication and follow up, someone isn't getting the job done, I'll want to know why. If there's no good reason, then I'll get impatient and angry...and take appropriate steps from there. But if you hire good people, motivate them to strive for excellence and then follow up constantly, it almost never gets to that state."

If you are feisty by nature and/or the position calls for a tough straw boss.

"You know what makes me angry? People who (the fill in the blanks with the most objectionable traits for this type of position)...people who don't pull their own weight, who are negative, people who lie...etc."

Question 26 Why aren't you earning more money at this stage of your career?

TRAPS: You don't want to give the impression that money is not important to you, yet you want to explain why your salary may be a little below industry standards.

BEST ANSWER: You like to make money, but other factors are even more important.

Example: "Making money is very important to me, and one reason I'm here is because I'm looking to make more. Throughout my career, what's been even more important to me is doing work I really like to do at the kind of company I like and respect.

(Then be prepared to be specific about what your ideal position and company would be like, matching them as closely as possible to the opportunity at hand.

Question 27 Who has inspired you in your life and why?

TRAPS: The two traps here are unpreparedness and irrelevance. If you grope for an answer, it seems you've never been inspired. If you ramble about your high school basketball coach, you've wasted an opportunity to present qualities of great value to the company.

BEST ANSWER: Have a few heroes in mind, from your mental "Board of Directors" – Leaders in your industry, from history or anyone else who has been your mentor.

Be prepared to give examples of how their words, actions or teachings have helped inspire your achievements. As always, prepare an answer which highlights qualities that would be highly valuable in the position you are seeking.

Question 28 What was the toughest decision you ever had to make?

TRAPS: Giving an unprepared or irrelevant answer.

BEST ANSWER: Be prepared with a good example, explaining why the decision was difficult...the process you followed in reaching it...the courageous or effective way you carried it out...and the beneficial results.

Question 29 Tell me about the most boring job you've ever had.

TRAPS: You give a very memorable description of a very boring job. Result? You become associated with this boring job in the interviewer's mind.

BEST ANSWER: You have never allowed yourself to grow bored with a job and you can't understand it when others let themselves fall into that rut.

Example: "Perhaps I've been fortunate, but that I've never found myself bored with any job I have ever held. I've always enjoyed hard work. As with actors who feel there are no small parts, I also believe that in every company or department there are exciting challenges and intriguing problems crying out for energetic and enthusiastic solutions. If you're bored, it's probably because you're not challenging yourself to tackle those problems right under your nose."

Question 30 Have you been absent from work more than a few days in any previous position?

TRAPS: If you've had a problem, you can't lie. You could easily be found out. Yet admitting an attendance problem could raise many flags.

BEST ANSWER: If you have had *no* problem, emphasize your excellent and consistent attendance record throughout your career.

Also describe how important you believe such consistent attendance is for a key executive...why it's up to you to set an example of dedication...and why there's just no substitute for being there with your people to keep the operation running smoothly, answer questions and handle problems and crises as they arise.

If you *do* have a past attendance problem, you want to minimize it, making it clear that it was an exceptional circumstance and that it's cause has been corrected.

To do this, give the same answer as above but preface it with something like, "Other that being out last year (or whenever) because of (your reason, which is now in the past), I have never had a problem and have enjoyed an excellent attendance record throughout my career. Furthermore, I believe, consistent attendance is important because..." (Pick up the rest of the answer as outlined above.).

Question 31 *What changes would you make if you came on board?*

TRAPS: Watch out! This question can derail your candidacy faster than a bomb on the tracks – and *just as you are about to be hired.*

Reason: No matter how bright you are, you cannot know the right actions to take in a position before you settle in and get to know the operation's strengths, weaknesses key people, financial condition, methods of operation, etc. If you lunge at this temptingly baited question, you will probably be seen as someone who shoots from the hip.

Moreover, no matter how comfortable you may feel with your interviewer, you are still an *outsider.* No one, including your interviewer, likes to think that a know-it-all outsider is going to come in, turn the place upside down and with sweeping, grand gestures, promptly demonstrate what jerks everybody's been for years.

BEST ANSWER: You, of course, will want to take a good hard look at everything the company is doing before making any recommendations.

Example: "Well, I wouldn't be a very good doctor if I gave my diagnosis *before* the examination. Should you hire me, as I hope you will, I'd want to take a good hard look at everything you're doing and understand why it's being done that way. I'd like to have in-depth meetings with you and the other key people to get a deeper grasp of what you feel you're doing right and what could be improved.

"From what you've told me so far, the areas of greatest concern to you are..." (name them. Then do two things. First, ask if these are in fact his major concerns. If so then reaffirm how your experience in meeting similar needs elsewhere might prove very helpful).

Question 32 I'm concerned that you don't have as much experience as we'd like in...

TRAPS: This could be a make-or-break question. The interviewer *mostly* likes what he sees, but has doubts over one key area. If you can assure him on this point, the job may be yours.

BEST ANSWER: This question is related to "The Fatal Flaw" (Question 18), but here the concern is not that you are *totally missing* some qualifications, such as CPA certification, but rather that your experience is *light* in one area.

Before going into any interview, try to identify the weakest aspects of your candidacy from this company's point of view. Then prepare the best answer you possible can to shore up your defenses.

To get past this question with flying colors, you are going to rely on your master strategy of *uncovering the employer's greatest wants and needs and then matching them with your strengths.* Since you already know how to do this from Question 1, you are in a much stronger position.

More specifically, when the interviewer poses as objection like this, you should...

Agree on the importance of this qualification.

Explain that your strength may be indeed be greater than your resume indicates because...

When this strength is added to your other strengths, it's really your *combination* of qualifications that's most important.

Then review the areas of your greatest strengths that match up most favorably with the company's most urgently-felt wants and needs.

This is powerful way to handle this question for two reasons. First, you're giving your interviewer more ammunition in the area of his concern. But more importantly, you're shifting his focus *away* from this one, isolated area and putting it on the *unique combination* of strengths you offer, strengths which tie in perfectly with his greatest wants.

Question 33 How do you feel about working nights and weekends?

TRAPS: Blurt out "no way, Jose" and you can kiss the job offer goodbye. But what if you have a family and want to work a reasonably normal schedule? Is there a way to get both the job and the schedule you want?

BEST ANSWER: First, if you're a confirmed workaholic, this question is a softball lob. Whack it out of the park on the first swing by saying this kind of schedule is just your style. Add that your family understands it. Indeed, they're happy for you, as they know you get your greatest satisfaction from your work.

If however, you prefer a more balanced lifestyle, answer this question with another: *"What's the norm for your best people here?"*

If the hours still sound unrealistic for you, ask, "Do you have any top people who perform exceptionally for you, but who also have families and like to get home in time to see them at night?" Chances are this company does, and this associates you with this other "top-performers-who-leave-not-later-than-six" group.

Depending on the answer, be honest about how you would fit into the picture. If all those extra hours make you uncomfortable, say so, but phrase your response positively.

Example: "I love my work and do it exceptionally well. I think the results speak for themselves, especially in ...(mention your two or three qualifications of greater interest to the employer. Remember, this is what he wants most, not a workaholic with *weak* credentials). Not only would I bring these qualities, but I've built my whole career on working not just hard, but *smart*. I think you'll find me one of the most *productive* people here.

I *do* have a family who likes to see me after work and on weekends. They add balance and richness to my life, which in turn helps me be happy and productive at work. If I could handle some of the extra work at home in the evenings or on weekends, that would be ideal. You'd be getting a person of exceptional productivity who meets your needs with strong credentials. And I'd be able to handle some of the heavy workload at home where I can be under the same roof as my family. Everybody would win."

Question 34 Are you willing to relocate or travel?

TRAPS: Answer with a flat "no" and you may slam the door shut on this opportunity. But what if you'd really prefer not to relocate or travel, yet wouldn't want to lose the job offer over it?

BEST ANSWER: First find out where you may have to relocate and how much travel may be involved. Then respond to the question.

If there's no problem, say so enthusiastically.

If you do have a reservation, there are two schools of thought on how to handle it.

One advises you to keep your options open and your reservations to yourself in the early going, by saying, "no problem". You strategy here is to get the best offer you can, then make a judgment whether it's worth it to you to relocate or travel.

Also, by the time the offer comes through, you may have other offers and can make a more informed decision. Why kill of this opportunity before it has chance to blossom into something really special? And if you're a little more desperate three months from now, you might wish you hadn't slammed the door on relocating or traveling.

The second way to handle this question is to voice a reservation, but assert that you'd be open to relocating (or traveling) for the right opportunity.

The answering strategy you choose depends on how eager you are for the job. If you want to take no chances, choose the first approach.

If you want to play a little harder-to-get in hopes of generating a more enticing offer, choose the second.

Question 35 Do you have the stomach to fire people? Have you had experience firing many people?

TRAPS: This "innocent" question could be a trap door which sends you down a chute and lands you in a heap of dust outside the front door. Why? Because its real intent is not just to see if you've got the stomach to fire, but also to uncover *poor judgment in hiring* which has caused you to fire so many. Also, if you fire so often, you could be a tyrant.

So don't rise to the bait by boasting how many you've fired, unless you've prepared to explain why it was beyond your control, and not the result of your poor hiring procedures or foul temperament.

BEST ANSWER: Describe the rational and sensible management process you follow in both hiring and firing.

Example: "My whole management approach is to hire the best people I can find, train them thoroughly and well, get them excited and proud to be part of our team, and then work with them to achieve our goals together. If you do all of that right, especially hiring the right people, I've found you don't have to fire very often.

"So with me, firing is a last resort. But when it's got to be done, it's got to be done, and the faster and cleaner, the better. A poor employee can wreak terrible damage in undermining the morale of an entire team of good people. When there's no other way, I've found it's better for all concerned to act decisively in getting rid of offenders who won't change their ways."

Question 36 Why have you had so many jobs?

TRAPS: Your interviewer fears you may leave this position quickly, as you have others. He's concerned you may be unstable, or a "problem person" who can't get along with others.

BEST ANSWER: First, before you even get to the interview stage, you should try to minimize your image as job hopper. If there are several entries on your resume of less than one year, consider eliminating the less important ones. Perhaps you can specify the time you spent at previous positions in *rounded years* not in months and years.

Example: Instead of showing three positions this way:

6/1982 – 3/1983, Position A;
4/1983 – 12/1983, Position B;
1/1984 – 8/1987, Position C;

...it would be better to show simply:

1982 – 1983, Position A;
1984 – 1987 Position C.

In other words, you would drop Position B altogether. Notice what a difference this makes in reducing your image as a job hopper.

Once in front of the interviewer and this question comes up, you must try to reassure him. Describe each position as part of an overall pattern of growth and career destination.

Be careful not to blame other people for your frequent changes. But you can and should attribute certain changes to conditions beyond your control.

Example: Thanks to an upcoming merger, you wanted to avoid an ensuing bloodbath, so you made a good, upward career move before your department came under the axe of the new owners.

If possible, also show that your job changes were more frequent in your younger days, while you were establishing yourself, rounding out your skills and looking for the right career path. At this stage in your career, you're certainly much more interested in the best *long-term* opportunity.

You might also cite the job(s) where you stayed the longest and describe that this type of situation is what you're looking for now.

Question 37 What do you see as the proper role/mission of...
...a good (job title you're seeking);
...a good manager;
...an executive in serving the community;
...a leading company in our industry; etc.

TRAPS: These and other "proper role" questions are designed to test your understanding of your place in the bigger picture of your department, company, community and profession....as well as the proper role each of these entities should play in *its* bigger picture.

The question is most frequently asked by the most *thoughtful* individuals and companies...or by those concerned that you're coming from a place with a radically different corporate culture (such as from a big government bureaucracy to an aggressive small company).

The most frequent mistake executives make in answering is simply not being prepared (seeming as if they've never giving any of this a though.)...or in phrasing an answer best suited to their *prior* organization's culture instead of the hiring company's.

BEST ANSWER: Think of the most essential ingredients of success for each category above – your job title, your role as manager, your firm's role, etc.

Identify at least three but no more than six qualities you feel are most important to success in each role. Then commit your response to memory.

Here, again, the more information you've already drawn out about the greatest wants and needs of the interviewer, and the more homework you've done to identify the culture of the firm, the more on-target your answer will be.

Question 38 What would you say to your boss if he's crazy about an idea, but you think it stinks?

TRAPS: This is another question that pits two values, in this case loyalty and honesty, against one another.

BEST ANSWER: Remember the rule stated earlier: In any conflict between values, *always choose integrity.*

Example: I believe that when evaluating anything, it's important to emphasize the positive. What do I like about this idea?"

"Then, if you have reservations, I certainly want to point them out, as specifically, objectively and factually as I can."

"After all, the most important thing I owe my boss is *honesty.* If he can't count on me for that, then everything else I may do or say could be questionable in his eyes."

"But I also want to express my thoughts in a constructive way. So my goal in this case would be to see if my boss and I could make his idea even stronger and more appealing, so that it effectively overcomes any initial reservation I or others may have about it."

"Of course, if he overrules me and says, 'no, let's do it my way,' then I owe him my full and enthusiastic support to make it work as best it can."

Question 39 How could you have improved your career progress?

TRAPS: This is another variation on the question, "If you could, how would you live your life over?" Remember, you're not going to fall for any such invitations to rewrite person history. You can't win if you do.

BEST ANSWER: You're generally quite happy with your career progress. Maybe, if you had known something earlier in life (impossible to know at the time, such as the booming growth in a branch in your industry...or the corporate downsizing that would phase out your last job), you might have moved in a certain direction sooner.

But all things considered, you take responsibility for where you are, how you've gotten there, where you are going...and you harbor no regrets.

Question 40 What would you do if a fellow executive on your own corporate level wasn't pulling his/her weight...and this was hurting your department?

TRAPS: This question and other hypothetical ones test your sense of human relations and how you might handle office politics.

BEST ANSWER: Try to gauge the political style of the firm and be guided accordingly. In general, fall back on universal principles of effective human relations – which in the end, embody the way you would like to be treated in a similar circumstance.

Example: "Good human relations would call for me to go directly to the person and explain the situation, to try to enlist his help in a constructive, positive solution. If I sensed resistance, I would be as persuasive as I know how to explain the benefits we can all gain from working together, and the problems we, the company and our customers will experience if we don't."

POSSIBLE FOLLOW-UP QUESTION: And what would you do if he still did not change his ways?

ANSWER: "One thing I wouldn't do is let the problem slide, because it would only get worse and overlooking it would set a bad precedent. I would try again and again and again, in whatever way I could, to solve the problem, involving wider and wider circles of people, both above and below the offending executive and including my own boss if necessary, so that everyone involved can see the rewards for teamwork and the drawbacks of non-cooperation."

"I might add that I've never yet come across a situation that couldn't be resolved by harnessing others in a determined, constructive effort."

Question 41 You've been with your firm a long time. Won't it be hard switching to a new company?

TRAPS: Your interviewer is worried that this old dog will find it hard to learn new tricks.

BEST ANSWER: To overcome this objection, you must point to the many ways you have grown and adapted to changing conditions at your present firm. It has *not* been a static situation. Highlight the different responsibilities you've held, the wide array of new situations you've faced and conquered.

As a result, you've learned to adapt quickly to whatever is thrown at you, and you thrive on the stimulation of new challenges.

To further assure the interviewer, describe the similarities between the new position and your prior one. Explain that you should be quite comfortable working there, since their needs and your skills make a perfect match.

Question 42 May I contact your present employer for a reference?

TRAPS: If you're trying to keep your job search private, this is the last thing you want. But if you don't cooperate, won't you seem as if you're trying to hide something?

BEST ANSWER: Express your concern that you'd like to keep your job search private, but that in time, it will be perfectly okay.

Example: "My present employer is not aware of my job search and, for obvious reasons; I'd prefer to keep it that way. I'd be most appreciative if we kept our discussion confidential right now. Of course, when we both agree the time is right, then by all means you should contact them. I'm very proud of my record there.

Question 43 *Give me an example of your creativity (analytical skill...managing ability, etc.)*

TRAPS: The worst offense here is simply being unprepared. Your hesitation may seem as if you're having a hard time remembering the last time you were creative, analytical, etc.

BEST ANSWER: Remember from Question 2 that you should commit to memory a list of your greatest and most recent achievements, ever ready on the tip of your tongue.

If you have such a list, it's easy to present any of your achievements in light of the quality the interviewer is asking about. For example, the smashing success you orchestrated at last year's trade show could be used as an example of creativity, or analytical ability, or your ability to manage.

Question 44 *Where could you use some improvement?*

TRAPS: Another tricky way to get you to admit weaknesses. Don't fall for it.

BEST ANSWER: Keep this answer, like all your answers, positive. A good way to answer this question is to identify a cutting-edge branch of your profession (one that's not essential to your employer's needs) as an area you're very excited about and want to explore more fully over the next six months.

Question 45 What do you worry about?

TRAPS: Admit to worrying and you could sound like a loser. Saying you never worry doesn't sound credible.

BEST ANSWER: Redefine the word 'worry' so that it does not reflect negatively on you.

Example: "I wouldn't call it worry, but I am a strongly goal-oriented person. So I keep turning over in my mind anything that seems to be keeping me from achieving those goals, until I find a solution. That's part of my tenacity, I suppose."

Question 46 How many hours a week do you normally work?

TRAPS: You don't want to give a specific number. Make it to low, and you may not measure up. Too high, and you'll forever feel guilty about sneaking out the door at 5:15.

BEST ANSWER: *If you are in fact a workaholic and you sense this company would like that:* Say you are a confirmed workaholic, that you often work nights and weekends. Your family accepts this because it makes you fulfilled.

If you are not a workaholic: Say you have always worked hard and put in long hours. It goes with the territory. It one sense, it's hard to keep track of the hours because your work is a labor of love, you enjoy nothing more than solving problems. So you're almost *always* thinking about your work, including times when you're home, while shaving in the morning, while commuting, etc.

Question 47 What's the most difficult part of being a (job title)?

TRAPS: Unless you phrase your answer properly, your interviewer may conclude that whatever you identify as "difficult" is where you are weak.

BEST ANSWER: First, redefine "difficult" to be "challenging" which is more positive. Then, identify an area everyone in your profession considers challenging and in which you excel. Describe the process you follow that enables you to get splendid results...and be specific about those results.

Example: "I think every sales manager finds it challenging to motivate the troops in a recession. But that's probably the strongest test of a top sales manager. I feel this is one area where I excel."

"When I see the first sign that sales may slip or that sales force motivation is flagging because of a downturn in the economy, here's the plan I put into action immediately..." (followed by a description of each step in the process...and *most importantly,* the exceptional results you've achieved.).

Question 48 The "Hypothetical Problem"

TRAPS: Sometimes an interviewer will describe a difficult situation and ask, *"How would you handle this?"* Since it is virtually impossible to have all the facts in front of you from such a short presentation, don't fall into the trap of trying to solve this problem and giving your verdict on the spot. It will make your decision-making process seem woefully inadequate.

BEST ANSWER: Instead, describe the rational, methodical process you would follow in analyzing this problem, who you would consult with, generating possible solutions, choosing the best course of action, and monitoring the results.

Remember, in all such, *"What would you do?"* questions, always describe your *process or working methods,* and you'll never go wrong.

Question 49 What was the toughest challenge you've ever faced?

TRAPS: Being unprepared or citing an example from so early in your life that it doesn't score many points for you at this stage of your career.

BEST ANSWER: This is an easy question if you're prepared. Have a recent example ready that demonstrates either:

A quality most important to the job at hand; or

A quality that is *always* in demand, such as leadership, initiative, managerial skill, persuasiveness, courage, persistence, intelligence, etc.

Question 50 Have you consider starting your own business?

TRAPS: If you say "yes" and elaborate enthusiastically, you could be perceived as a loose cannon in a larger company, too entrepreneurial to make a good team player...or someone who had to settle for the corporate life because you couldn't make a go of your own business.

Also too much enthusiasm in answering "yes" could rouse the paranoia of a small company indicating that you may plan to go out on your own soon, perhaps taking some key accounts or trade secrets with you.

On the other hand, if you answer "no, never" you could be perceived as a security-minded drone who never dreamed a big dream.

BEST ANSWER: Again it's best to:

Gauge this company's corporate culture before answering and...

Be honest (which doesn't mean you have to vividly share your fantasy of the franchise or bed-and-breakfast you someday plan to open).

In general, if the corporate culture is that of a large, formal, military-style structure, minimize any indication that you'd love to have your own business. You might say, "Oh, I may have given it a thought once or twice, but my whole career has been in larger organizations. That's where I have excelled and where I want to be."

If the corporate culture is closer to the free-wheeling, everybody's-a-deal-maker variety, then emphasize that in a firm like this, you can virtually get the best of all worlds, the excitement of seeing your own ideas and plans take shape...combined with the resources and stability of a well-established organization. Sounds like the perfect environment to you.

In any case, no matter what the corporate culture, be sure to indicate that any desires about running your own show are part of your *past*, not your present or future.

The last thing you want to project is an image of either a dreamer who failed and is now settling for the corporate cocoon...or the restless maverick who will fly out the door with key accounts, contacts and trade secrets under his arms just as soon as his bankroll has gotten rebuilt.

Always remember: Match what you want with what the position offers. The more information you've uncovered about the position, the more believable you can make your case.

Question 51 What are your goals?

TRAPS: Not having any...or having only vague generalities, not *highly specific* goals.

BEST ANSWER: Many executives in a position to hire you are strong believers in goal-setting. (It's one of the reason they've achieved so much). They like to hire in kind.

If you're vague about your career and personal goals, it could be a big turnoff to may people you will encounter in your job search.

Be ready to discuss your goals for each major area of your life: career, personal development and learning, family, physical (health), community service and (if your interviewer is clearly a religious person) you could briefly and generally allude to your spiritual goals (showing you are a well-rounded individual with your values in the right order).

Be prepared to describe each goal in terms of specific milestones you wish to accomplish along the way, time periods you're allotting for accomplishment, why the goal is important to you, and the specific steps you're taking to bring it about. But do this concisely, as you never want to talk more than two minutes straight before letting your interviewer back into the conversation.

Question 52 *What do you for when you hire people?*

TRAPS: Being unprepared for the question.

BEST ANSWER: Speak your own thoughts here, but for the best answer weave them around the three most important qualifications for *any* position.

Can the person do the work (qualifications)?

Will the person do the work (motivation)?

Will the person fit in ("our kind of team player")?

Question 53 Sell me this stapler...(this pencil...this clock...or some other object on interviewer's desk).

TRAPS: Some interviewers, especially business owners and hard-changing executives in marketing-driven companies, feel that good salesmanship is *essential* for any key position and ask for an instant demonstration of your skill. Be ready.

BEST ANSWER: Of course, you already know the most important secret of all great salesmanship – *"find out what people want, then show them how to get it."*

If your interviewer picks up his stapler and asks, "sell this to me," you are going to demonstrate this proven master principle. *Here's how:*

"Well, a good salesman must know both his product and his prospect before he sells anything. If I were selling this, I'd first get to know everything I could about it, all its features and benefits."

"Then, if my goal were to sell it _you_, I would do some research on how you might use a fine stapler like this. The best way to do that is by asking some questions. May I ask you a few questions?"

Then ask a few questions such as, "Just out of curiosity, if you didn't already have a stapler like this, why would you want one? And in addition to that? Any other reason? Anything else?"

"And would you want such a stapler to be reliable?...Hold a good supply of staples?" (Ask more questions that point to the features this stapler has.)

Once you've asked these questions, make your presentation citing all the features and benefits of this stapler and why it's exactly what the interviewer just told you he's looking for.

Then close with, "Just out of curiosity, what would you consider a reasonable price for a quality stapler like this...a stapler you could have *right now* and would (then repeat all the problems the stapler would solve for him)? Whatever he says, (unless it's zero), say, "Okay, we've got a deal."

NOTE: If your interviewer tests you by *fighting* every step of the way, denying that he even wants such an item, *don't fight him.* Take the product away from him by saying, "Mr. Prospect, I'm delighted you've told me right upfront that there's no way you'd ever want this stapler. As you well know, the first rule of the most productive salespeople in any field is to meet the needs of people who really *need and want* our products, and it just wastes everyone's time if we try to force it on those who don't. And I certainly wouldn't want to waste your time. But we sell many items. Is there *any* product on this desk you would very much like to own...just one item?" When he points something out, repeat the process above. If he knows anything about selling, he may give you a standing ovation.

Question 54 "The Salary Question" – How much money do you want?

TRAPS: May also be phrases as, *"What salary are you worth?"*...or, *"How much are you making now?"* This is your most important negotiation. Handle it wrong and you can blow the job offer or go to work at far less than you might have gotten.

BEST ANSWER: For maximum salary negotiating power, remember these five guidelines:

Never bring up salary. Let the interviewer do it first. Good salespeople sell their products thoroughly before talking price. *So should you.* Make the interviewer want you first, and your bargaining position will be much stronger.

If your interviewer raises the salary question too early, before you've had a chance to create desire for your qualifications, *postpone* the question, saying something like, "Money is important to me, but is _not_ my main concern. Opportunity and growth are far more important. What I'd rather do, if you don't mind, is explore if I'm right for the position, and then talk about money. Would that be okay?"

The #1 rule of any negotiation is: *the side with more information wins.* After you've done a thorough job of selling the interviewer and it's time to talk salary, the secret is to get the employer talking about what he's willing to pay *before* you reveal what *you're* willing to accept. So, when asked about salary, respond by asking, "I'm sure the company has already established a salary range for this position. Could you tell me what that is?" Or, "I want an income commensurate with my ability and qualifications. I trust you'll be fair with me. What does the position pay?" Or, more simply, "What does this position pay?"

Know beforehand what you'd accept. To know what's reasonable, research the job market and this position for any relevant salary information. Remember that most executives look for a 20-25%$ pay boost when they switch jobs. If you're grossly underpaid, you may want more.

Never lie about what you currently make, but feel free to include the estimated cost of all your fringes, which could well tack on 25-50% more to your present "cash-only" salary.

Question 55 The Illegal Question

TRAPS: Illegal questions include any regarding your age...number and ages of your children or other dependents...marital status...maiden name...religion...political affiliation...ancestry...national origin...birthplace...naturalization of your parents, spouse or children...diseases...disabilities...clubs...or spouse's occupation...*unless any of the above are directly related to your performance of the job.* You can't even be asked about *arrests*, though you can be asked about *convictions.*

BEST ANSWER: Under the ever-present threat of lawsuits, most interviewers are well aware of these taboos. Yet you may encounter, usually on a second or third interview, a senior executive who doesn't interview much and forgets he can't ask such questions.

You can handle an illegal question in several ways. First, you can assert your legal right not to answer. But this will frighten or embarrass your interviewer and destroy any rapport you had.

Second, you could swallow your concerns over privacy and answer the question straight forwardly if you feel the answer could help you. For example, your interviewer, a devout Baptist, recognizes you from church and mentions it. Here, you could gain by talking about your church.

Third, if you don't want your privacy invaded, you can diplomatically answer the *concern* behind the question without answering the question itself.

Example: If you are over 50 and are asked, *"How old are you?"* you can answer with a friendly, smiling question of your own on whether there's a concern that your age my affect your performance. Follow this up by reassuring the interviewer that there's nothing in this job you can't do and, in fact, your age and experience are the most important *advantages* you offer the employer for the following reasons...

Another example: If asked, *"Do you plan to have children?"* you could answer, "I am wholeheartedly dedicated to my career", perhaps adding, "I have no plans regarding children." (You needn't fear you've pledged eternal childlessness. You have every right to change your plans later. Get the job first and then enjoy all your options.)

Most importantly, remember that illegal questions arise from fear that you won't perform well. The best answer of all is to get the job and perform brilliantly. All concerns and fears will then varnish, replaced by respect and appreciation for your work.

Question 56 The "Secret" Illegal Question

TRAPS: Much more frequent than the Illegal question *(see Question 55)* is the **secret** illegal question. It's secret because it's asked only in the interviewer's mind. Since it's not even expressed to you, you have no way to respond to it, and it can there be most damaging.

Example: You're physically challenged, or a single mother returning to your professional career, or over 50, or a member of an ethnic minority, or fit any of a dozen other categories that do not strictly conform to the majority in a given company.

Your interviewer wonders, "Is this person really able to handle the job?"..."Is he or she a 'good fit' at a place like ours?"..."Will the chemistry ever be right with someone like this?" But the interviewer never raises such questions because they're illegal. So what can you do?

BEST ANSWER: Remember that just because the interviewer doesn't ask an illegal question doesn't mean he doesn't have it. More than likely, he is going to come up with his own answer. So you might as well help him out.

How? Well, you obviously can't respond to an illegal question if he hasn't even asked. This may well offend him. And there's always the chance he wasn't even concerned about the issue until you brought it up, and only then begins to wonder.

So you can't address "secret" illegal questions *head-on.* But what you can do is make sure there's enough *counterbalancing* information to more than reassure him that there's no problem in the area he *may* be doubtful about.

For example, let's say you're a sales rep who had polio as a child and you need a cane to walk. You know your condition has never impeded your performance, yet you're concerned that your interviewer may secretly be wondering about your stamina or ability to travel. Well, make sure that you hit these abilities very hard, leaving no doubt about your capacity to handle them well.

So, too, if you're in any different from what passes for "normal". Make sure, without in any way seeming *defensive* about yourself that you mention strengths, accomplishments, preferences and affiliations that strongly counterbalance any unspoken concern your interviewer may have.

Question 57 What was the toughest part of your last job?

TRAPS: This is slightly different from the question raised earlier, *"What's the most difficult part of being a (job title...)"* because this asks what you *personally* have found most difficult in your last position. This question is more difficult to redefine into something positive. Your interviewer will assume that whatever you found toughest may give you a problem in your new position.

BEST ANSWER: State that there was nothing in your prior position that you found overly difficult, and let your answer go at that. If pressed to expand your answer, you could describe the aspects of the position you *enjoyed* more than others, making sure that you express maximum enjoyment for those tasks most important to the open position, and you enjoyed least those tasks that are unimportant to the position at hand.

Question 58 How do you define success...and how do you measure up to your own definition?

TRAPS: Seems like an obvious enough question. Yet many executives, unprepared for it, fumble the ball.

BEST ANSWER: Give a well-accepted definition of success that leads right into your own stellar collection of achievements.

Example: "The best definition I've come across is that success is the progressive realization of a worthy goal."

"As to how I would measure up to that definition, I would consider myself both successful and fortunate..."(Then summarize your career goals and how your achievements have indeed represented a progressive path toward realization of your goals.)

Question 59 "The Opinion Question" – What do you think about ...Abortion...The President...The Death Penalty...(or any other controversial subject)?

TRAPS: Obviously, these and other "opinion" questions should never be asked. Sometimes they come up over a combination dinner/interview when the interviewer has had a drink or two, is feeling relaxed, and is spouting off about something that bugged him in today's news. If you give your opinion and it's the opposite of his, you won't change his opinions, but you could easily lose the job offer.

BEST ANSWER: In all of these instances, just remember the tale about student and the wise old rabbi. The scene is a seminary, where an overly serious student is pressing the rabbi to answer the ultimate questions of suffering, life and death. But no matter how hard he presses, the wise old rabbi will only answer each difficult question with a question of his own.

In exasperation, the seminary student demands, "Why, rabbi, do you always answer a question with another question?" To which the rabbi responds, "And why not?"

If you are ever uncomfortable with *any* question, asking a question in return is the greatest escape hatch ever invented. It throws the onus back on the other person, sidetracks the discussion from going into an area of risk to you, and gives you time to think of your answer or, even better, *your next question!*

In response to any of the "opinion" questions cited above, merely responding, *"Why do you ask?"* will usually be enough to dissipate any pressure to give your opinion. But if your interviewer again presses you for an opinion, you can ask another question.

Or you could assert a generality that almost everyone would agree with. For example, if your interviewer is complaining about politicians then suddenly turns to you and asks if you're a

Republican or Democrat, you could respond by saying, "Actually, I'm finding it hard to find any politicians I like these days."

(Of course, your best question of all may be whether you want to work for someone opinionated.)

Question 60 If you won $10 million lottery, would you still work?

TRAPS: Your totally honest response might be, *"Hell, no, are you serious?"* That might be so, but any answer which shows you as fleeing work if given the chance could make you seem lazy. On the other hand, if you answer, *"Oh, I'd want to keep doing exactly what I am doing, only doing it for your firm,"* you could easily inspire your interviewer to silently mutter to himself, *"Yeah, sure. Gimme a break."*

BEST ANSWER: This type of question is aimed at getting at your bedrock attitude about work and how you feel about what you do. Your best answer will focus on your positive feelings.

Example: "After I floated down from cloud nine, I think I would still hold my basic belief that achievement and purposeful work are essential to a happy, productive life. After all, if money alone bought happiness, then all rich people would be all happy, and that's not true.

"I love the work I do, and I think I'd always want to be involved in my career in some fashion. Winning the lottery would make it more fun because it would mean having more flexibility, more options...who knows?"

"Of course, since I can't count on winning, I'd just as soon create my own destiny by sticking with what's worked for me, meaning good old reliable hard work and a desire to achieve. I think those qualities have built many more fortunes that all the lotteries put together."

Question 61 Looking back on your last position, have you done your best work?

TRAPS: Tricky question. Answer *"absolutely"* and it can seem like your best work is behind you. Answer, *"no, my best work is ahead of me,"* and it can seem as if you didn't give it your all.

BEST ANSWER: To cover both possible paths this question can take, your answer should state that you always try to do your best, and the best of your career is right now. Like an athlete at the top of his game, you are just hitting your career stride thanks to several factors. Then, recap those factors, highlighting your strongest qualifications.

Question 62 Why should I hire you from the outside when I could promote someone from within?

TRAPS: This question isn't as aggressive as it sounds. It represents the interviewer's own dilemma over this common problem. He's probably leaning toward you already and for reassurance, wants to hear what you have to say on the matter.

BEST ANSWER: Help him see the qualifications that *only* you can offer. You should speak confidently and honestly about your abilities. But you should avoid sounding overly boastful

Example: "In general, I think it's a good policy to hire from within – to look outside probably means you're not completely comfortable choosing someone from inside.

"Naturally, you want this department to be as strong as it possibly can be, so you want the strongest candidate. I feel that I can fill that bill because...(then recap your strongest qualifications that match up with his greatest needs)."

Question 63 Tell me something negative you've heard about our company...

TRAPS: This is a common fishing expedition to see what the industry grapevine may be saying about the company. But it's also a trap because as an outsider, you never want to be the bearer of unflattering news or gossip about the firm. It can only hurt your chances and sidetrack the interviewer from getting sold on you.

BEST ANSWER: Just remember the rule – never be negative – and you'll handle this one just fine.

Question 64 On a scale of one to ten, rate me as an interviewer.

TRAPS: Give a perfect "10," and you'll seem too easy to please. Give anything less than a perfect 10, and he could press you as to where you're being critical, and that road leads *downhill* for you.

BEST ANSWER: Once again, *never be negative.* The interviewer will only resent criticism coming from you. This is the time to show your positivism.

However, don't give a numerical rating. Simply praise whatever interview style he's been using.

If he's been tough, say "You have been thorough and tough-minded, the very qualities needed to conduct a good interview."

If he's been methodical, say, "You have been very methodical and analytical, and I'm sure that approach results in excellent hires for your firm."

In other words, pay him a sincere compliment *that he can believe* because it's anchored in the behavior you've just seen.

Question 65 Are you a team player?

TRAPS: You are, of course, a team player.

BEST ANSWER: Be sure to have examples ready. Specifics that show you often perform for the good of the team rather than for yourself are good evidence of your team attitude.

Do not brag, just say it in a matter-of-fact tone. This is a key point.

Good luck in your job search!